100 WAYS TO DEAL WITH ABSENTEEISM IN SCHOOLS

DR DHEERAJ MEHROTRA

Contents

Preface

The widespread problem of school absenteeism impacts students, teachers, and the educational system as a whole. It harms kids' learning, academic performance, and well-being in the long run. Despite how common it is, there is no one solution to student absenteeism; instead, it requires a multipronged strategy to address the wide range of causes.

For school administrators, teachers, and lawmakers who are serious about raising attendance rates and creating welcoming learning environments, "100 Ways to Deal With Absenteeism in Schools" is an exhaustive resource. This book provides objective, evidence-based answers that can be applied to many contexts and challenges. It goes beyond being a mere collection of methods.

I hope that teachers will be better able to help their pupils when we provide them with the tools they need to succeed. By applying these tactics, schools may foster an inclusive community where all students feel respected, encouraged, and driven to show up consistently. I am sure this book will be invaluable in your fight against student absenteeism and for a better education for all.

www.authordheerajmehrotra.com

ᐅᐅᐅ

ONE

100 WAYS TO DEAL WITH ABSENTEEISM IN SCHOOLS

―♡―

Importance of Attendance in Schools:

Attending school is essential to academic progress and student development. Students learn important ideas and participate in class discussions with regular attendance. Cognitive development and academic success require this constant interaction. When youngsters consistently refuse to attend school, this behaviour is called school avoidance or refusal. This condition can occur as a result of emotional turmoil brought on by bullying, educational expectations, family issues, or mental health challenges such as anxiety and depression. It is necessary to take a multi-pronged approach to address school avoidance. The creation of an atmosphere that is encouraging is an essential component. In the context of the entire world, between two to five per cent of students are absent from school.

Attendance also improves social skills and relationships. Regular school attendance helps students develop communication and teamwork skills by interacting with peers and teachers. These relationships foster a pleasant school climate and a sense of belonging, which is essential for mental health.

Consistent attendance teaches students discipline and responsibility, preparing them for professional contexts that require regular attendance. It also develops routines and time management skills for personal and academic success.

High attendance rates improve school performance and effectiveness. Schools with higher attendance rates receive more funds and resources, improving instruction.

Frequent attendance is essential for academic success, social, emotional, life skills development, and educational and career success. Parents are providing their children with electronic devices, and children are more interested in attending coaching centres than schools that strongly focus on discipline. The best way for parents to get around this scenario is to play movies in front of them that demonstrate what occurs when they are working with other students, what happens when more and more kids work together, how cooperation is the key to success, and how it develops a network. A network for alumni can also be established with the help of this network.

Although addressing the issue of school avoidance can be a problematic and multi-faceted challenge, if the appropriate tactics are utilized, it is feasible to assist pupils in overcoming their worries and returning to the classroom. As a result of the huge rise in absenteeism and school avoidance over the past few years, academic performance has been completely negatively impacted. School avoidance is a frustrating behavior that can become a habitual pattern for some adolescents, which can be frustrating for parents, caregivers, and teachers. This avoidance leads to missing assignments and social estrangement, which in turn creates anxiety about going back to school and may ultimately lead to an increase in absenteeism. There are a number of factors that contribute to this issue, including the rise in the number of parents working from home, the rise in anxiety and mental health problems, and the changes in attendance policies that have occurred after COVID.

Let us learn about the various ways to ensure Absenteeism in Schools.

ᗞᗞᗞ

Initiate discussions without getting angry. Initiate calm, respectful conversations with kids to foster understanding and problem-solving without anger, creating a positive school environment.

⊳⊳⊳

Listen properly and understand why the child does not want to attend school.

⊳⊳⊳

Discuss this with the class teacher, supervisor, and school counsellor.

⊳⊳⊳

Prepare a plan of action for gradual re-entry to school.

⊳⊳⊳

Acquiring an Understanding of and Comprehending the Issue
Establish open contact lines with the students to understand their feelings and worries during the learning experience.

⊳⊳⊳

Keep an eye on the student's conduct and look for indications that they are experiencing anxiety or distress as a result of their schoolwork.

ᐅᐅᐅ

Help the student discover the exact triggers that drive them to avoid school by working together with them to identify these triggers.

ᐅᐅᐅ

Gather Information: It is essential to speak with the student's teachers, counsellors, and parents to obtain complete information about their circumstances.

ᐅᐅᐅ

Check-ins on Emotional Well-Being: Regularly verifying the student's emotional health is essential.

ᐅᐅᐅ

The school administration must formulate anti-bullying rules and make mental health services available. Preventing school avoidance can also

involve establishing a constructive environment, implementing mental health programs, encouraging parental involvement, and providing flexible learning options.

▷▷▷

Setting Building an Atmosphere That Is Encouragement. Listen attentively to understand the child's reasons for avoiding school, showing

empathy and support to address their concerns and encourage a positive school experience.

ÞÞÞ

Safe area: If a student feels overwhelmed, a secure area should be accessible at school. Establishing a safe location at school for overwhelmed students has shown positive progress. Students are utilizing this space to regain composure, reduce stress, and improve their overall well-being and academic performance.

ÞÞÞ

Acknowledge that every student's experience of school refusal is different. Collaborate with the student, the student's family, and any other specialists pertinent to the situation to create a customized strategy.

ÞÞÞ

It is recommended that students begin with half-day attendance before moving on to full-day attendance. This gradual approach helps students acclimate, manage anxiety, and build confidence before moving to full-day attendance.

ᐅᐅᐅ

It may also require implementing a flexible learning program, which may involve modifications to the curriculum, a reduced amount of homework assigned, or additional academic help.

ᐅᐅᐅ

Rewarding attendance and working with positive reinforcement is a productive way to motivate and encourage employees. Rewarding attendance and using positive reinforcement effectively motivates and encourages employees. Recognizing their commitment fosters a positive work environment, enhances morale, and promotes consistent attendance and productivity.

ᐅᐅᐅ

Regular Routine: Establishing a regular daily

routine is vital to offering stability. Consistent schedules help students feel secure, enhance time management skills, and improve overall academic and behavioural outcomes.

ᐳᐳᐳ

Support from Peers: Foster friendships and provide support from peers. Fostering friendships and giving peer support are crucial for a positive school

experience. Strong peer relationships enhance social skills, boost self-esteem, and create a supportive network, encouraging regular attendance and engagement in school activities.

⊳⊳⊳

Involvement of the Family: Involve the family in establishing a supportive atmosphere within the house. When families are engaged, they can reinforce routines, provide encouragement, and address any challenges their child may face, fostering a positive environment that supports learning and consistent school attendance. This collaboration strengthens the child's sense of belonging and educational commitment.

⊳⊳⊳

Assistance and Interventions from Professionals as motivation for kids to come to school. Providing aid and interventions from professionals can motivate kids to go to school by addressing their individual needs and challenges. These professionals offer support tailored to the student's situation, whether it's academic, emotional, or behavioural, thereby helping to create a positive and inclusive school environment where every student feels valued and supported in their educational journey.

⊳⊳⊳

Please encourage students to seek extra support from the school counsellor by referring them to this resource. This initiative aims to provide personalized assistance and guidance, fostering emotional well-being and academic success.

ᚦᚦᚦ

If avoidance behaviours are severe, seeking professional counselling is essential. Professional counsellors can provide specialized support and interventions to address underlying issues effectively, promoting a positive and successful school experience for the student.

ᚦᚦᚦ

Implement tailored behavioural interventions to meet students' specific needs. These interventions should be carefully designed to effectively address individual challenges, promote positive behavioural changes, and support the student's academic and personal development.

ᚦᚦᚦ

Providing instruction in social skills is crucial to helping learners become more comfortable with social interactions. These skills include communication, empathy, cooperation, and conflict resolution, which foster positive relationships and enhance the overall school experience for students.

ᗵᗵᗵ

Addressing fears beneath the surface using cognitive-behavioral therapy (CBT) techniques is effective. By identifying and challenging negative thought patterns, CBT helps students manage anxiety, build resilience, and develop coping strategies, promoting a more positive and confident approach to school and social interactions.

ᗵᗵᗵ

Make the student's workload more manageable by adjusting assignments and tasks based on their needs and capabilities. This approach ensures that students can succeed academically without feeling overwhelmed, fostering a positive learning environment conducive to their well-being.

ᗵᗵᗵ

Flexible scheduling or part-time attendance is an option that should be considered. Once a plan is established, it's crucial to communicate regularly with the student and their family. This ensures that

everyone stays informed about the student's progress at school and allows for any necessary adjustments to the plan.

ϷϷϷ

Provide tutoring support to help students catch up on missed work. This personalized assistance ensures that students receive targeted help in understanding concepts and completing

assignments, promoting academic success and reducing stress associated with falling behind.

❧❧❧

Offering alternative assignments aligned with students' interests is beneficial. It promotes engagement and motivation by allowing them to apply skills and knowledge in ways that resonate with their passions, enhances learning outcomes, and fosters a positive attitude towards schoolwork.

❧❧❧

Implementing learning accommodations whenever necessary is crucial to support students' individual needs. These accommodations may include adjusted assignments, extended time for tests, or assistive technology, ensuring that all students have equal opportunities to succeed academically and participate fully in the learning process.

❧❧❧

Instructing students on coping strategies to manage stress and anxiety is essential for their well-being. Teaching techniques such as deep breathing, mindfulness exercises, time management skills, and positive self-talk empower students to handle challenges effectively, promoting resilience and a positive mindset in academic and personal situations.

ᐅᐅᐅ

Empowering students involves developing their problem-solving skills. Teaching strategies like analyzing situations, brainstorming solutions, and evaluating outcomes fosters independence and critical thinking. These skills equip students to tackle challenges effectively, build confidence, and succeed academically and personally.

ᐅᐅᐅ

Incorporating mindfulness exercises into students' daily routines benefits their overall well-being. These practices, such as deep breathing, guided meditation, or mindful movement, help students manage stress, improve focus, and enhance emotional regulation. By cultivating mindfulness, students develop resilience and a positive mindset, which supports their academic success and mental health.

ᐅᐅᐅ

Participating in activities that enhance self-esteem and confidence is essential for personal growth. These activities include setting achievable goals, practising self-care, cultivating positive relationships, and celebrating achievements. These efforts promote self-awareness, resilience, and a healthy self-image, contributing to overall well-being and success in various aspects of life.

ᗡᗡᗡ

Goal setting involves creating realistic and manageable objectives that learners can strive to achieve. This process helps students clarify their priorities, stay motivated, and track progress effectively. By setting attainable goals, students develop a sense of purpose and direction and foster continuous growth and success in their academic and personal endeavours.

ᗡᗡᗡ

Providing professional training for parents is crucial to empower them to support their children effectively. This training should focus on understanding child development, communication strategies, positive discipline techniques, and ways to foster a supportive home environment conducive to learning. By equipping parents with knowledge and skills, schools can enhance collaboration between home and school, ultimately promoting students' academic success and well-being.

ᗡᗡᗡ

Ensuring regular updates to parents about their child's progress is vital for fostering effective communication and partnership between home and school. Parents can actively support their child's educational journey by providing timely information on academic achievements, behavioural developments, and areas needing improvement. This transparency helps maintain trust, encourages parental involvement, and ensures that parents and educators are aligned in supporting the student's overall growth and success.

ᐅᐅᐅ

To encourage their children to go to school, parents can use a variety of strategies that are beneficial at home, including the following:

Establish a Routine: Make it a habit to maintain a morning routine that consists of getting up at the appropriate time, eating a nutritious breakfast, and getting ready for school.

▷▷▷

Encourage children to attend school consistently by providing them with positive reinforcement through praise and awards for high attendance. These rewards could include additional playtime or a little treat.

▷▷▷

Maintaining open and supportive communication with your kid about their feelings and experiences at school and addressing any concerns they may have is an essential part of parenting.

▷▷▷

Establish Attendance objectives: Collaborate with your child to establish attainable attendance objectives and celebrate their accomplishments when they reach these goals.

ppp

Ensure that your child's school supplies are prepared the night before, and cultivate a positive and encouraging environment at home regarding school attendance. This will help you build a welcoming environment for your child.

ppp

If your child complains about not wanting to go to school, you should have a conversation with them to understand the factors driving their feelings and then work together to address any fears or anxiety that they may have.

ppp

Participate in School Activities: Establish a solid

relationship with the teachers and staff at your child's school by participating in parent-teacher conferences and keeping yourself updated on the activities and events that are taking place there.

ᐳᐳᐳ

By continuously adopting these strategies at home, parents can help instil a favourable attitude about school attendance in their children, promoting academic performance and overall well-being.

ᐳᐳᐳ

A collaborative approach between home and school ensures that parents and educators work together towards a child's academic and personal success. Open communication, shared goals, and active parent involvement create a supportive environment for learning. Consistency in expectations and problem-solving fosters a positive school experience and reinforces the importance of attendance and engagement. This partnership enhances the child's overall development and prepares them for future challenges.

ᐳᐳᐳ

Reviewing and modifying attendance policies to be encouraging is crucial for promoting student engagement and success. Policies should consider flexible attendance options, supportive interventions for frequent absences, and positive reinforcement for regular attendance. By creating policies prioritising student well-being and participation, schools can foster a positive culture around attendance and ensure all students have equitable opportunities to thrive academically and socially.

❦❦❦

Implementing and enforcing anti-bullying measures is crucial for fostering a safe school environment. Clear policies, staff training, and proactive monitoring are essential. Promoting awareness and community involvement strengthens efforts against bullying. By prioritizing prevention and support, schools can ensure a respectful and inclusive atmosphere where all students thrive.

❦❦❦

Prompt action should be taken whenever signs indicate a student is avoiding school. This includes understanding the reasons behind the avoidance, offering support, and collaborating with parents and educators to address the underlying issues effectively. Early intervention helps prevent further disengagement and supports the student's well-being and academic success.

꧁꧂

Clear communication among all stakeholders is crucial for effective collaboration and understanding. Establishing transparent channels ensures that information flows efficiently between parents, teachers, students, and administrators. This clarity fosters a supportive environment where concerns can be addressed promptly, goals can be aligned, and decisions can be made collaboratively to benefit the entire school community.

꧁꧂

Regular follow-ups are essential to assess progress and make necessary adjustments. By consistently evaluating outcomes, schools can ensure that interventions effectively support students and improve outcomes. This ongoing assessment helps to refine strategies, address emerging challenges, and maintain momentum towards achieving academic and personal growth goals for all students.

꧁꧂

Interest-based learning engages students by integrating their interests into the curriculum. Educators can enhance motivation, participation, and knowledge retention by connecting course content with what students find personally meaningful. This approach fosters active learning and deeper engagement and encourages students to take ownership of their learning journey, ultimately promoting a more fulfilling educational experience.

༄༄༄

Encouraging students to participate in extracurricular activities enriches their overall educational experience. These activities foster teamwork, leadership skills, and personal development beyond academic learning. By engaging in sports, clubs, arts, or community service, students build social connections, discover new interests, and cultivate a well-rounded perspective that enhances their academic success and prepares them for future endeavours.

༄༄༄

Incorporating student voices into educational decisions fosters a supportive and inclusive learning environment. Schools promote autonomy, responsibility, and a sense of ownership among students by empowering them to make decisions that impact their education. This approach enhances student engagement and motivation and ensures that educational practices are responsive to learners' diverse needs and perspectives, ultimately contributing to their academic success and personal

development.

PPP

Engaging learners with creative projects is an effective strategy for maintaining their interest and enhancing learning. Educators can stimulate students' curiosity, critical thinking, and problem-solving skills by incorporating hands-on activities, multimedia presentations, and collaborative tasks. This approach encourages active participation, deepens understanding of concepts, and fosters creativity, making learning enjoyable and meaningful for learners.

PPP

Motivational interviews are crucial for understanding and addressing concerns effectively. Educators can use this technique to engage students in open and supportive conversations to explore their motivations, aspirations, and challenges. This approach helps build trust, clarify goals, and empower students to take ownership of their learning journey. Through motivational interviews, educators can provide personalized support, foster resilience, and cultivate a positive mindset conducive to academic and personal growth.

PPP

Promoting good sleep hygiene practices is essential for maintaining physical health. Encouraging consistent sleep schedules, limiting screen time before bed, creating a comfortable sleep environment, and practising relaxation techniques can improve sleep quality. Adequate rest supports overall well-being, enhances cognitive function, and boosts energy levels, ensuring students are ready to engage and learn effectively during school hours.

ϷϷϷ

Ensuring students maintain a healthy diet is crucial for their overall well-being and academic performance. Encouraging balanced meals that include fruits, vegetables, lean proteins, and whole grains supports physical health and cognitive function. Educators and parents can promote nutrition education, provide access to nutritious food options, and model healthy eating habits to instil lifelong wellness practices in students. A nutritious diet helps students stay focused, energized, and ready to learn in school.

ϷϷϷ

Encouraging regular physical activity is vital for promoting overall health and well-being. Encouraging students to engage in activities such as sports, outdoor play, or fitness classes supports physical fitness, enhances mood, and reduces stress. Educators can incorporate physical activity breaks into the school day, promote active transportation, and emphasize the importance of movement for maintaining a healthy lifestyle. By fostering a culture of physical activity, schools contribute to students' physical development, mental clarity, and overall academic success.

ÞÞÞ

Medical Checkups: It's important to schedule regular checkups with the visiting doctor to monitor the health, catch potential issues early, and maintain the students' overall well-being. These routine checkups help ensure that any developing conditions are identified and addressed promptly, preventing more serious health problems in the future. Regular visits also allow one to discuss health concerns and receive tailored advice on maintaining a healthy lifestyle. Prioritizing these checkups is essential for students' proactive health management.

ÞÞÞ

Managing Stress: Teaching students various ways to manage stress, such as deep breathing exercises, mindfulness practices, time management techniques, and seeking support from peers and adults, promotes emotional resilience and helps them cope effectively with academic and personal challenges.

ᐯᐯᐯ

Enhancing the quality of the educational experience involves improving curriculum relevance, using innovative teaching methods, fostering a supportive environment, personalizing learning, and continually refining educational practices based on feedback and data. This approach ensures students receive a robust education that prepares them for future challenges and opportunities.

ᐯᐯᐯ

Promote cultural diversity, implement anti-bullying policies, engage the community, support staff empathy, and empower student leadership to create a welcoming and inclusive school atmosphere. This will ensure a supportive environment where all students thrive.

ᐯᐯᐯ

Encouraging excellent relationships between teaching and administrative staff fosters a cohesive school community. Clear communication, mutual respect, and collaboration enhance efficiency and morale. Strong relationships create a supportive environment where ideas are shared, challenges are addressed effectively, and collective goals are pursued to benefit students' academic and personal growth.

ᗞᗞᗞ

Incorporating fun and exciting activities during the school day enhances student engagement, motivation, and overall learning experience. These activities can include interactive lessons, educational games, group projects, and hands-on experiments. Educators can inspire curiosity, creativity, and active student participation by making learning enjoyable and fostering a positive

and stimulating classroom environment.

ᗅᗅᗅ

Organizing field trips enhances learning by providing real-world experiences that complement classroom instruction. These trips allow students to explore new environments, apply academic concepts, and engage in hands-on learning. Field trips promote curiosity, critical thinking, and cultural awareness while fostering social skills and teamwork. By connecting classroom learning to the outside world, educators create memorable and impactful learning opportunities that inspire and motivate students.

ᗅᗅᗅ

Including students in school festivities and activities enriches their school experience by fostering a sense of belonging and community. Participation in sports days, cultural celebrations, talent shows, and academic competitions promotes social interaction, teamwork, and personal growth. It also encourages students to showcase their talents, develop confidence, and form positive relationships with peers and teachers. Educators create a vibrant and supportive learning environment that enhances student engagement and well-being by actively involving students in school activities.

ᗅᗅᗅ

Tracking a student's development and adjusting strategies is essential for personalized learning and growth. By regularly assessing academic progress, social-emotional well-being, and learning needs, educators can tailor instructional approaches to support individual strengths and areas for improvement. This proactive approach ensures that students receive the necessary support and resources to achieve their full potential. Continuous monitoring allows for timely interventions, fosters student success, and promotes a positive learning experience.

ÞÞÞ

Establishing a feedback loop with learners is crucial for understanding their perspectives, learning preferences, and challenges. This continuous exchange of feedback allows educators to adjust teaching methods, content delivery, and support strategies based on student insights. By actively listening to student feedback, educators can create a more responsive and personalized learning environment that promotes engagement, motivation, and academic growth. This collaborative approach enhances communication, fosters trust, and empowers students to take ownership of their learning journey.

ÞÞÞ

Adaptability and readiness to modify teaching techniques in response to students' changing needs are essential for effective education. Flexibility allows educators to tailor instruction, support, and resources to meet individual learning styles, challenges, and interests. Educators can foster a dynamic and responsive learning environment that adapts to change and promotes student engagement, motivation, and success. This approach ensures that teaching practices remain relevant and effective in addressing evolving educational demands and supporting students in reaching their academic goals.

ᐅᐅᐅ

Conducting frequent evaluations of students' progress is essential for assessing their academic achievements and understanding their strengths and areas needing improvement. Regular assessments help educators tailor instruction, provide targeted support, and track individual growth. Educators can make informed decisions to effectively enhance teaching strategies and meet students' educational needs by continuously monitoring student performance and learning outcomes. This proactive approach supports student success by ensuring learning experiences are personalized, engaging, and aligned with academic goals.

ᐅᐅᐅ

Celebrating even the most minor victories is crucial for building momentum. Recognizing students' academic, social, or personal achievements fosters a positive learning environment and boosts morale. By acknowledging accomplishments, educators encourage continuous effort, perseverance, and a growth mindset among students. Celebrations can range from verbal praise and certificates to group acknowledgements and special activities, reinforcing the value of hard work and progress. This practice motivates students and strengthens their self-confidence and resilience, contributing to long-term academic success and well-being.

ᐅᐅᐅ

Gradual exposure to the school's surroundings is a critical component of exposure therapy for students experiencing anxiety or school avoidance. This process involves systematically introducing the student to different aspects of the school environment in a controlled and supportive manner. Starting with less intimidating areas or situations, the student can gradually build comfort and confidence, progressing to more challenging settings. This approach helps reduce anxiety, fosters familiarity and promotes a sense of safety within the school. By carefully increasing exposure, educators and therapists can support the student's adjustment and reintegration into the school community.

ᐅᐅᐅ

Role-playing is an effective way to practice and enhance social interaction skills. Students can develop their communication abilities, empathy, and problem-solving strategies by simulating real-life scenarios in a safe and supportive environment. This method allows learners to experiment with different responses, receive feedback, and gain confidence in their social interactions. Through role-playing, students can better prepare for various social situations, improving their ability to navigate relationships and collaborate with peers.

ᐅᐅᐅ

Instructors should teach students specific techniques for handling anxiety to encourage school attendance. Deep breathing, mindfulness, and muscle relaxation can help students manage stress. Positive visualization and cognitive behavioural strategies can shift their mindset towards more positive thoughts about school. Encouraging regular physical activity and maintaining a healthy lifestyle also supports anxiety reduction. These techniques empower students to cope with their anxiety and improve their school attendance.

ᐅᐅᐅ

Facilitating the formation of support groups for students facing similar challenges can be highly beneficial. These groups provide a safe space for students to share their experiences and offer mutual support. Students can feel less isolated and more understood by connecting with peers who understand their struggles. Support groups can also promote the exchange of coping strategies and foster community. This collective support can significantly aid in managing their challenges and improving their overall well-being.

ᐅᐅᐅ

Pairing students with mentors through mentoring programs can be incredibly impactful. Mentors provide guidance, support, and encouragement, helping students navigate academic and personal challenges. This relationship can boost the student's confidence, motivation, and resilience. Mentors can also offer valuable insights and advice based on their own experiences. Mentoring programs can foster a positive and supportive environment that promotes student growth and success.

ᐅᐅᐅ

When assigning tasks, choosing ones that interest the student can significantly enhance engagement and motivation. Students are likelier to invest effort and enthusiasm into enjoyable or relevant activities. This approach also helps develop a positive attitude towards learning and can improve academic performance. Additionally, incorporating their interests can make learning more meaningful and personalized. Ultimately, this strategy fosters a more dynamic and practical educational experience.

ᐧᐧᐧ

Providing leadership opportunities can significantly boost students' self-assurance. Taking on leadership roles allows students to develop critical skills such as decision-making, communication, and responsibility. These experiences can enhance their confidence and sense of capability. Leadership opportunities also help students understand the value of teamwork and the importance of setting a positive example for peers. Ultimately, fostering leadership in students prepares them for future challenges and success.

ᐧᐧᐧ

Involving students in community service projects can be highly beneficial. Such engagement promotes a sense of responsibility and empathy as students contribute to the welfare of others. It also provides practical experiences that enhance their problem-solving and teamwork skills. Community service can boost students' self-esteem by allowing them to see the tangible impact of their efforts. Overall, it fosters a strong connection to the community and helps students develop into well-rounded, socially

conscious individuals.

ᐅᐅᐅ

Assigning students positions of responsibility within the classroom can foster a sense of ownership and accountability. Depending on the student's strengths and interests, these roles include tasks like class monitor, peer tutor, or group leader. Responsibilities promote leadership skills, teamwork, and organization, enhancing the student's learning experience. Moreover, they instil pride and accomplishment as students contribute actively to the classroom environment. Assigning responsibilities can also improve behaviour and engagement by giving students a stake in the classroom dynamics.

ᐅᐅᐅ

Implementing a buddy system can provide students with invaluable support from peers. Pairing them with a buddy fosters friendships, reduces feelings of isolation, and promotes a sense of belonging. This system encourages student collaboration and cooperation, enhancing social skills and empathy. Buddies can also offer academic assistance, share experiences, and provide emotional support, creating a supportive and inclusive learning environment. The buddy system nurtures positive relationships and contributes to students' well-being and success.

ᐅᐅᐅ

Supporting students who are nervous about public speaking is crucial for their development. Offering techniques such as practice sessions, constructive feedback, and relaxation exercises can build their confidence over time. Encouraging a supportive classroom environment where mistakes are seen as opportunities for growth can alleviate anxiety. Providing individualized attention and gradual exposure to public speaking can help students overcome their fears. Nurturing their skills in a supportive setting prepares them for future academic and professional challenges.

ᐅᐅᐅ

Students can employ several effective strategies to overcome test anxiety. Deep breathing exercises, positive visualization, and time management skills can help manage stress. Encouraging regular study habits, practising relaxation before exams, and maintaining a balanced lifestyle are also beneficial. Providing a supportive and encouraging environment in the classroom can further alleviate anxiety. Ultimately, equipping students with these methods empowers them to approach tests and perform at their best confidently.

ᐅᐅᐅ

Addressing social anxiety involves employing targeted strategies to help students feel more comfortable in social situations. Techniques such as gradual exposure, role-playing, and teaching social skills can build confidence. Encouraging positive self-talk, setting realistic expectations, and fostering a supportive peer environment are also effective. Providing opportunities for students to practice social interactions in a safe and structured manner can significantly reduce anxiety. Ultimately, these strategies empower students to navigate social settings more quickly and confidently.

ᗡᗡᗡ

Assisting younger pupils with separation anxiety is crucial for their emotional development and academic success. Implementing strategies such as gradual separation, reassuring routines, and building trust with caregivers can help ease their anxiety. Creating a nurturing environment where children feel safe and supported is essential. Educators can also collaborate closely with parents to ensure consistency between home and school. Addressing separation anxiety sensitively fosters a positive school experience and promotes healthy social-emotional growth in younger students.

ᗡᗡᗡ

Teaching students techniques for coping with performance anxiety is essential for their overall development. Methods such as deep breathing exercises, visualization, and positive self-talk can help manage anxiety levels. Providing opportunities for practice and constructive feedback can also build confidence. Educators should create a supportive environment where students feel encouraged to take risks and learn from mistakes. Ultimately, teaching coping techniques empowers students to navigate challenging situations with resilience and self-assurance.

ᐳᐳᐳ

Teaching students how to advocate for themselves through self-advocacy is empowering and essential for their growth. It involves helping them understand their strengths, weaknesses, and needs and teaching them how to articulate these effectively. By fostering self-awareness and teaching communication skills, students learn to assert their rights and seek support when needed. Educators can facilitate this process by providing opportunities for practice, role-playing scenarios, and offering guidance on problem-solving. Ultimately, self-advocacy equips students with lifelong skills to navigate challenges confidently and advocate for their academic and personal well-being.

ᐳᐳᐳ

Including students in the decision-making process fosters a sense of ownership and responsibility in their education. It empowers them to voice their opinions, contribute ideas, and feel valued within the school community. This practice enhances engagement, motivation, and a more profound commitment to their learning. Students develop critical thinking, leadership, and collaborative skills by actively participating. Ultimately, involving students in decision-making nurtures a more

inclusive and dynamic educational environment, promoting mutual respect and a stronger sense of community.

ᐁᐁᐁ

Developing skills for independence is crucial for students as it prepares them for future challenges. Encourage self-management by teaching time management and organizational skills. Promote critical thinking and problem-solving abilities to enable students to make informed decisions. Foster self-confidence through tasks that require initiative and responsibility. Additionally, support the development of practical life skills, such as financial literacy and essential self-care, to further enhance their independence. These skills empower students to navigate life's demands confidently and competently.

ᐁᐁᐁ

Assigning obligations that encourage independence is integral to fostering student responsibility. By giving them tasks that require self-management, decision-making, and accountability, students learn to rely on their abilities and judgment. This process helps them develop essential life skills, such as time management, problem-solving, and self-discipline. Additionally, experiencing the consequences of their actions teaches them the value of responsibility. Ultimately, these opportunities promote personal growth, confidence, and a sense of autonomy, preparing students for future challenges.

ᐅᐅᐅ

Teaching students efficient time management skills is crucial for academic success and personal development. Educators can start by helping students create a daily schedule that includes time for studying, extracurricular activities, and relaxation. Introducing tools such as planners, calendars, and to-do lists can assist students in organizing their tasks and prioritizing their responsibilities. Additionally, teaching techniques like setting specific goals, breaking tasks into manageable steps, and avoiding procrastination can further enhance their ability to manage time effectively. Students can balance their activities, reduce stress, and improve their productivity by mastering time management.

ᐅᐅᐅ

Implementing collaboration-based learning strategies is an effective way to enhance student learning and engagement. Collaborative learning encourages students to collaborate, share ideas, and solve problems collectively. This approach can be facilitated through group projects, peer teaching, and interactive discussions. Students develop critical skills such as communication, teamwork, and conflict resolution by working in teams. They also gain diverse perspectives, which can deepen their understanding of the subject. Additionally, collaboration fosters a supportive learning environment where students can motivate and learn from each other, ultimately leading to a more enriching educational experience.

❧❧❧

Assigning team assignments is an excellent strategy to develop social skills among students. Working in teams requires students to communicate effectively, share responsibilities, and collaborate towards a common goal. Through this process, they learn essential skills such as active listening, negotiating, and giving and receiving constructive feedback. Team assignments also encourage students to respect diverse perspectives and manage conflicts amicably. Students build trust and camaraderie by engaging in group tasks, which can enhance their overall learning experience. Ultimately, these collaborative efforts prepare students for future professional environments where teamwork is crucial.

❧❧❧

Peer learning is a powerful educational approach that fosters mutual support and knowledge exchange among students. Encouraging students to learn from and teach each other helps to create a collaborative classroom environment. Peer learning can be facilitated through group discussions, study partnerships, peer tutoring, and collaborative projects. This method allows students to gain different perspectives, clarify their understanding, and reinforce their learning by teaching concepts to others. Additionally, peer support can boost confidence, motivation, and a sense of community within the classroom. Educators can enhance student engagement and deepen their understanding of the material by promoting peer learning.

ppp

It is essential to collaborate closely with parents when working with them as partners. Building solid and communicative relationships fosters a supportive environment for students. This partnership ensures that parents are actively involved in their child's education, providing valuable insights and reinforcing learning at home. Regular updates and open communication help align school and home strategies, promoting consistency and a unified approach to the child's development.

ppp

It's essential to utilize the community resources available to provide further assistance and support the development of individual students in the school. Community resources such as counselling services, extracurricular programs, and vocational training can supplement school initiatives, offering diverse student growth and enrichment opportunities. Collaborating with local organizations strengthens the educational experience by addressing specific needs and fostering a supportive environment conducive to academic and personal success. This partnership empowers students with various resources and opportunities contributing to their overall development and well-being.

▷▷▷

Encouraging students' interests and hobbies outside school is crucial for their development. It helps them explore their passions, build confidence, and develop essential life skills. By supporting activities like sports, arts, clubs, and community involvement, schools can foster well-rounded individuals who are motivated and engaged inside and outside the classroom. This approach enhances students' academic performance and nurtures their creativity, social skills, and emotional well-being, contributing to a balanced and fulfilling educational experience.

PPP

Encouraging students to pursue passion initiatives is crucial for personal development and academic success. When students engage in activities they are passionate about, they tend to show more extraordinary dedication, creativity, and perseverance. These initiatives can include projects, clubs, sports, arts, or community service activities that align with their interests and goals. By fostering a supportive environment that values and nurtures student passions, schools can inspire lifelong learning and cultivate well-rounded individuals who are motivated to excel both inside and outside the classroom. This approach enhances student engagement and promotes a positive school culture where students feel empowered to explore their talents and make meaningful contributions to their communities.

PPP

Providing opportunities for career exploration is crucial for students to gain insights into various professions, industries, and career pathways. Students can discover their interests, strengths, and potential career paths by engaging in career exploration activities such as job shadowing, internships, career fairs, and guest speaker sessions. These experiences allow students to make informed decisions about their future careers, understand the skills and qualifications required in different fields, and explore real-world workplace environments. Career exploration also helps students develop critical thinking, decision-making, and networking skills, preparing them for success in their future academic and professional endeavours. Overall, integrating career exploration into education empowers students to set goals, pursue their aspirations, and align their scholarly pursuits with their career ambitions.

ᐅᐅᐅ

Fostering self-reflection and personal development is essential in nurturing students' growth and maturity. By encouraging self-reflection, educators empower students to examine their strengths, weaknesses, values, and goals. This reflective process enables them to understand themselves better, their motivations, and their aspirations. Through self-reflection, students can identify areas for improvement, set realistic goals, and develop strategies to achieve them. It also cultivates self-

awareness, resilience, and adaptability, crucial skills for lifelong learning and personal success. By incorporating self-reflection into education, schools support academic growth and promote holistic development, preparing students to navigate challenges, make informed decisions, and thrive in their personal and professional lives.

▷▷▷

Mind Maps and Fishbone Diagrams are valuable tools in classrooms for fostering a constructive mindset among students. Mind Maps visually organize information, encouraging students to connect ideas, identify relationships, and see the bigger picture of concepts. This helps enhance critical thinking, problem-solving skills, and creativity by allowing students to explore various perspectives and brainstorm ideas effectively.

On the other hand, Fish Bone Diagrams, also known as Ishikawa diagrams, are used to analyze cause-and-effect relationships. They help students break down complex issues or problems into manageable components, identify root causes, and understand how different factors interconnect to influence outcomes. Using these diagrams, students develop analytical skills, structure their thoughts logically, and approach challenges methodically.

These visual tools promote active learning, engagement, and collaboration in the classroom.

They empower students to organize information, make connections, and think critically, fostering a constructive mindset supporting their academic and personal growth.

ᐅᐅᐅ

Positive affirmations are powerful tools for building self-assurance and cultivating a positive mindset. By consistently repeating positive statements about oneself or one's abilities, individuals can reinforce self-belief, boost confidence, and overcome self-doubt. These affirmations act as mental reinforcements, reshaping negative thought patterns into constructive ones, promoting resilience and a proactive approach to challenges.

Positive affirmations can be particularly beneficial for students in educational settings. When students affirm their strengths, capabilities, and potential for success, they develop a more optimistic outlook on their academic abilities. This can lead to improved motivation, enhanced academic performance, and a greater willingness to take on new challenges. Moreover, positive affirmations create a supportive and encouraging classroom environment where students feel empowered to strive for their goals.

Teachers and educators are crucial in promoting positive affirmations among students by integrating them into daily routines, such as morning meetings or before assessments. By encouraging students to affirm their strengths and abilities, educators help foster a mindset of growth and self-efficacy, ultimately nurturing confident and resilient learners.

ÞÞÞ

Visualization is a valuable tool for students to enhance goal clarity, reduce anxiety, and improve performance by mentally rehearsing desired outcomes. It fosters creativity, problem-solving skills, and integration with learning processes, making it an effective strategy in education.

ÞÞÞ

Implementing gratitude practices can significantly enhance students' overall well-being by fostering positive emotions, improving relationships, and reducing stress. Schools can cultivate a supportive and optimistic atmosphere conducive to learning and personal growth by incorporating activities like gratitude journaling or sharing thankful moments.

ÞÞÞ

Encouraging a growth mindset fosters resilience, persistence, and a belief in improving through effort and learning. It shifts focus from fixed abilities to continuous development, empowering students to embrace challenges and learn from setbacks, ultimately enhancing their academic and personal

achievements.

ᑭᑭᑭ

Positive role models play a crucial role in shaping individuals' behaviours, attitudes, and aspirations. Introducing them to a group can inspire and motivate them, providing examples of success, perseverance, and ethical conduct. This exposure helps cultivate positive values, self-confidence, and a sense of direction, benefiting personal growth and community development.

ᑭᑭᑭ

Providing students with instruction on emotional regulation skills is essential for their overall well-being. These skills enable students to manage stress, navigate challenges, and maintain positive relationships. By learning techniques such as deep breathing, mindfulness, and identifying emotions, students can develop resilience and cope effectively with various situations they encounter in school and beyond. Emotional support and regulation education significantly create a supportive and conducive learning environment.

ᑭᑭᑭ

Encouraging students to express their feelings safely and constructively is crucial for their emotional development. By creating an environment where students feel heard and understood, they can learn to communicate their emotions effectively. This can include activities like journaling, art, or group discussions, providing outlets that foster self-expression without judgment. Teaching students these skills helps build confidence, resilience, and healthy relationships, contributing to a positive

overall school experience.

ᐅᐅᐅ

Encouraging students to express their feelings safely and constructively is crucial for their emotional development. By creating an environment where students feel heard and understood, they can learn to communicate their emotions effectively. This can include activities like journaling, art, or group discussions, providing outlets that foster self-expression without judgment. Teaching students these skills helps build confidence, resilience, and healthy relationships, contributing to a positive overall school experience.

ᐅᐅᐅ

Establishing support networks within the institution is essential for fostering a supportive and nurturing student environment. These networks can include peer support groups, counselling services, mentoring programs, and collaborations with parents and community resources. By creating these networks, students can feel more connected, supported, and empowered to navigate challenges and achieve their academic and personal goals effectively. Support networks also promote a sense of belonging and well-being, contributing to a positive school culture where every student can thrive.

ᐅᐅᐅ

Validating students' experiences and feelings is crucial in creating a supportive and empathetic learning environment. When educators acknowledge and validate students' emotions, it helps build trust, enhances communication, and fosters a sense of belonging. This validation reassures students that their feelings are heard and respected, encouraging them to express themselves openly and seek support when needed. It also promotes emotional intelligence and resilience, equipping students with valuable skills to navigate challenges effectively and thrive academically and personally.

ᐁᐁᐁ

Continuous support and monitoring are essential to ensure students' well-being and academic success. Educators can identify challenges early and offer timely interventions by maintaining regular check-ins and providing consistent encouragement. This approach helps foster a supportive environment where students feel valued and motivated to engage actively in their learning journey. Additionally, continuous support enables educators to address any emerging issues promptly, adapt teaching strategies as needed, and collaborate with parents and other stakeholders to provide holistic support for students' development and achievement.

ᐁᐁᐁ

Implementing preventative measures involves identifying potential issues before they escalate and taking proactive steps to mitigate them. This approach can include creating clear policies and guidelines, conducting regular risk assessments, providing training and resources to staff and students, fostering a positive and respectful school climate, and promoting open communication channels. By addressing challenges preemptively, schools can create a safer and more supportive environment conducive to learning and growth for all students.

▷▷▷

Building resilience in students is crucial for their emotional and mental well-being. It involves teaching them skills to adapt to challenges, manage stress, and bounce back from setbacks. Strategies may include promoting positive thinking, encouraging problem-solving skills, fostering supportive relationships, providing opportunities for growth and learning from failures, and teaching effective coping mechanisms. By cultivating resilience, students can develop the confidence and strength to navigate adversity and thrive academically and personally.

▷▷▷

A holistic approach to a student's well-being involves comprehensively addressing their physical, emotional, social, and academic needs. It means recognizing that health, family dynamics, peer relationships, and school environment impact their development and success. By considering these elements together, educators and caregivers can create supportive environments that foster holistic growth and well-being in students. This approach aims to nurture academic achievement, emotional resilience, social skills, physical health, and a positive sense of self-worth.

❧❧❧

Creating a warm and encouraging atmosphere in schools is crucial for helping children overcome school avoidance and thrive holistically. Schools can effectively address and mitigate school avoidance behaviours by implementing supportive measures such as mentoring programs, counselling services, positive reinforcement for attendance, and involving parents in the process. This approach supports academic success and promotes emotional well-being and social development, ensuring that students feel

valued, supported, and motivated to engage actively in their educational journey.

About The Author

Dheeraj Mehrotra, MS, MPhil, PhD (Education Management)., a white and a yellow belt in SIX SIGMA, a Certified NLP Business Diploma holder, is an Educational Innovator, Author, with expertise in Six Sigma In Education, Academic Audits, Neuro-Linguistic Programming (NLP), Total Quality Management In Education, an Experiential Educator, a CBSE Resource towards School Assessment (SQAA), CCE, JIT, Five S, and KAIZEN. He has authored over 100 books on computer science, AI, digital body language, NLP, quality circles, school management, classroom effectiveness, and safety and security. A former Principal at De Indian Public School, New Delhi, (INDIA), NPS International School, Guwahati, and Education Officer at GEMS, Gurgaon, with ample teaching experience of over Three Decades, he is a certified Trainer for Quality Circles/ TQM in Education and QCI Standards for School Accreditation/ School Audits and Management. He has also been honoured with the President of India's National Teacher Award in 2006 and the Best Science Teacher State Award (By the Ministry of Science and Technology, State of UP), Innovation in Education for his inception of Six Sigma In Education by Education Watch, New Delhi and Education World- Best Teacher Award, BOLT Learner Teacher Award by Air India, 'Innovation in Education Award 2016' by Higher Education Forum (HEF), Gujarat Chapter, among others. He has developed over 150 FREE EDUCATIONAL MOBILE Apps for the Google Play Store exclusively for Teachers, Students, and Parents. This work has been recognised by the LIMCA BOOK OF RECORDS and INDIA BOOK OF RECORDS as the only Indian to draw that feast. As a founder president of the IoT Society of India, he also promotes Technology Globally. Dr Mehrotra is presently engaged as a PRINCIPAL at KUNWARS GLOBAL SCHOOL, Lucknow, India. He has conducted over 2000 workshops globally on "Excellence In Education" integrated with Total Quality Management and Six Sigma, Technology Integration in Education (TIE), Developing towards being ROCKSTAR TEACHERS, including Cyberspace, Cyber Security, Classroom Management, School Leadership & Management, and Innovative teaching within classrooms via Mind Maps, NLP and Experiential Learning in Academics. He is an active TEDx speaker and can be viewed on the YouTube TEDx channel. As a premium UDEMY Instructor, he has developed over 500 courses and caters to over 8 Lakh students from 180 countries. He can be visited at www.authordheerajmehrotra.com

www.authordheerajmehrotra.com

Books By The Same Author

Books

Cyber Security
For Kids
2022

Classroom
Teaching Ideas
2022

BASICS OF
ARTIFICIAL...
2019

Smart Career
Planner
2020

Student
Engagement...
2022

Marketing
Mantras For...
2021

Tools And Tips
For Teaching...
2021

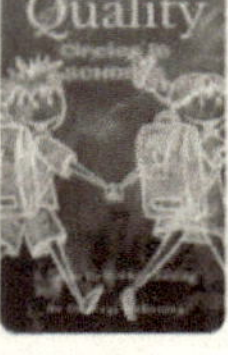

Quality Circles
in Schools
2022

Basics of
Artificial...
2021

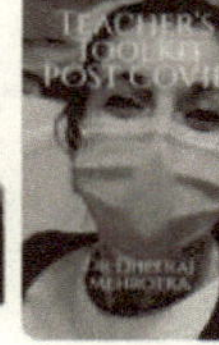

Teacher's
Toolkit Post...
2021

AI Basics for
School...
2019

Basics of Go
Programming
2022

Optimising Educational...

2022

High Performance...

2020

Learning Beyond COVID

2022

Secrets to Raising a...

2022

101 SCHOOL MANAGEME...

2017

Digital Body Language

2020

The Quality Icon

2022

Academic Quality...

2022

The One Minute Educator

2021

Digital Wellbeing For...

2022

The 64 Kalas of Krishna For...

2023

Risk Management...

2022

R Programming
For Beginners
2021

Impact of
Information...
2021

Pedagogical
Practices to...
2022

Motivating &
Quality...
2022

Child
Safeguarding ...
2022

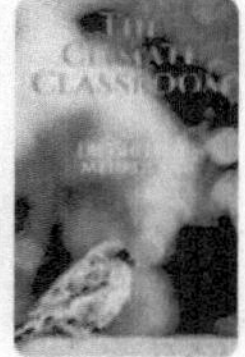

Climate
Classroom
2021

NEP 2020- At a
Glance for...
2021

Street Smart
Teaching...
2021

Optimal Child
Development
2022

Roadmap To A
New Normal...
2020

Teaching in a
Digital Age
2022

Conscious
Parenting
2021

School

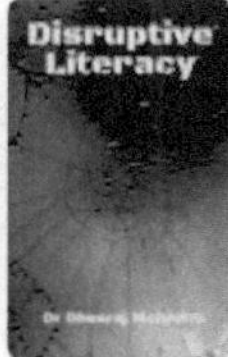

Disruptive

Ways to

100 Ideas For

100 Green

Academic